How To Start a Food Truck

By J.H. Dies

A Newbiz Playbook Publication

For downloadable tools emailed directly to you please email **products@newbizplaybook.com** use the password foodtruckpro in the re: of the email

For my family, the answer to my why

Chapter 1. Is The Food Truck Business for You?

Introduction

So you're thinking of starting a food truck? Congratulations! The food truck business is booming, and it is providing incredible opportunities for young entrepreneurs to test concepts, and expand brands beyond for wheels to mini restaurant empires. If this is what you have in mind, welcome aboard. We are here to help!

The food truck business isn't exactly new in the market, but the number of food trucks has increased from the year 2007 to 2012 as many street food lovers prefer to eat their food outdoors and on the go. In fact, a market research report made by the IBISWorld showed that from 2011-2016, there was another remarkable rise in the industry as a whole with a total generated revenue of $870m and also an annual growth of 7.9% in each of those 5 years.

Where you make your money in the food truck business may also surprise some new business owners. The IBISWorld study also showed that 55% of total sales were found in street corners while 18% were from events. About 15% were from construction sites, with the other 12% coming from shopping malls.

As you can see, the industry is a vastly growing one and is still continuing to grow steadily.

What exactly makes a food truck very appealing to the public? For one, most people, especially those working in dynamic fast paced urban environments don't have time to sit down and enjoy a meal. In a fast paced society like ours it isn't surprising to see people rushing to work, then rushing to lunch, and then rushing back to work again.

With this kind of lifestyle, it's hard to sit down and enjoy a steak. Hence, many people turn to food trucks because aside from the good food they serve, the variety of delicious offerings, and because they don't need to wait long to get their food. All of these reasons for the attraction to food trucks should factor into how you design and plan your food truck business. For example, if your proposed offerings are the sort that take long lead times, or will have customers waiting for their food, you should look to how to reduce the time from order, to service with advanced prep etcetera. Otherwise, your business will suffer, because its offerings are directly counter to what draws clients to your truck in the first place.

Secondly, food trucks traditionally serve food cheaper than most establishments because of the relatively low overhead. This is a major advantage you will have with your truck. However, you will want to find the sweet spot between being less expensive than a brick and mortar restaurant, and getting to margins that will help your business grow.

As compared to an actual establishment, food trucks demand less overhead (we'll go into the details of the expenses later) and no waiter or server charges. In a slowing economy, people tend to try to save as much money as they can to get by. With food trucks driving around, you can bet that people will opt for the cheaper choice instead of dining at an actual restaurant. Again this should play a role in your decision to include high cost items in your offerings. While you may have a great recipe with steak or lobster, you will want to be strategic with the options you offer on your menu, for folks who may not want to spend at that level.

For these reasons and more, we believe starting a food truck could be an excellent business opportunity. Later on in the book, we'll be discussing how to get started in a food truck business and what to do to keep it running.

Without further adieu, let's get started...

Chapter 1. Pros and Cons of the Food Truck Lifestyle

The food trucker lifestyle isn't exactly for everyone. If you're going to venture into this kind of business, then you have to be prepared to be very hands on, since food businesses, in general, need complete supervision, especially for startups. To further determine whether a food truck business is for you, let's go through the pros and the cons so that you can weigh each aspect and make a decision as to whether you'd want to pursue the venture or not.

Pros of Opening a Food Truck Business

1. Low Overhead Investments

As mentioned earlier, opening a food truck business requires relatively low overhead costs to start up as compared to a restaurant. All you need is a truck, a kitchen, equipment, inventory, and extra money for maintenance and gas. The rest can be spent on marketing and advertising. For the truck, you can actually rent food trucks for a fixed rate and add your own design as long as your decorations and art can be taken off. In fact, that is what you should do to test your concept, and a truck you are considering buying, before shelling out big cash. More about that later.

It is cheaper in the long run to buy your own truck, but for those who are low on budget, renting can be a good startup option. You also need a kitchen, sometimes called a commissary where food is prepared, prior to the business day. These are available for rent, but in the beginning, unless there is a need for commercial equipment, it is best to use your own kitchen. Why a kitchen? Newbies to the food truck business sometimes believe that food prep can easily be handled in the truck, or on a cook to order basis.

First, operation of food truck kitchen equipment is much more expensive than your own kitchen, whether it be propane for gas, or an electric generator fueled by gasoline on the truck. Second, a key to your success will be the speed at which you can serve each item on your menu. Thoughtful prep, should be used to in every possible way to reduce cooking and serving times. Long lines of people waiting on food will drive away customers.

Very successful food truck businesses evolve to a point, where there is a prep team, and sometimes even a runner who is constantly delivering pre-cut veggies, or extra supplies of sliced meat etc.

You will need kitchen equipment and supplies for preparing the food (e.g. stove, pots, pans etc.).

2. Easy to Get Customers

As compared to the regular food establishments, food trucks will usually go to their customers and not the other way around. For a typical restaurant, the establishment will wait for the customers to come. In the food business, there are peak hours and dead hours, with peak hours being the time with the most customers (usually during lunch and dinner time) and dead hours wherein there are little to no customers (usually after lunch or late afternoon when everyone is in the office).

The great thing about food trucks is that during dead hours, they can go around and look for business because they're mobile anyway, or they can use this time to prep for the next busy time, using a reduced staff. Your business won't have waiters sitting around waiting for a single late diner, and a manager overseeing them.

If the area where they're in doesn't have customers, they can look for another area with a lot of people, or call it a day. This opens up many opportunities for developing your business through marketing and other important planning. This is also a great strategy to get the words out about your business, getting you more potential customers in the long run.

3.   Easy for Catering

If you offer catering, then things will be easier for you. You don't need to hire delivery to ship all the food to the destination, since you can just use your food truck. You can store all of your food in the food truck and preserve it properly, while still bringing a product that is top quality because it didn't "sit" in a heater waiting to be served. You may even tie up with catering companies, who would want to make use of your truck for serving customers, when you are not running. The opportunities in the catering industry are ripe and wide. This should definitely be an early focus for growing revenue.

4.   Easy for Participating in Events

Food trucks can easily access in festivals or other public events and get more customers. If a certain event (like a carnival) is happening, you can tie up with the organizers of the carnival to grab a good spot there, and just park in a well located area serving tons of people. In fact, you don't even need to tie up with organizers at an event sometimes. You can just park your truck right outside the event, and the people will come to your truck. For instance, if there happens to be a concert, you can just park your truck near the entrance (if the organizers allow it). There are hundreds of people in line waiting to get in who are hungry or thirsty. You can take advantage of that kind of situation.

Cons of a Food Truck Business

1.   This is Still a Risky Business.

Done right, this business is still going to require up front outlay of material cash. Later, we will provide ideas for reducing these costs, and testing your concept to avoid a massive cash failure, but like all businesses, a number of food trucks do fail. Well planned trucks with good concepts, thrive, so that is what we must be.

2. Tough to Manage Inventory

One of the main disadvantages of having a food truck is that it is tough to manage inventory. Let's say that you've got a really good business day and customers finished up all your food inventory. If it's in the middle of the day and you still want to continue serving food, you either have to go back to your kitchen or get someone to deliver. On slower days, food can be wasted if customers are not there. This is why tracking sales, both to location, and on a per event basis is critical to managing your food costs.

3. Vague Regulations for Food Truck Businesses

Unlike regular restaurants, regulations for food truck businesses in some areas can be quite vague. There is temptation to skirt regulations, or shortcut certifications, but DO NOT do this. Health regulators regularly check food trucks, especially where they are gathered together in groups, and you do not want to deal with a shutdown at a critical time, and the major fines associated with failing to comply. The good news is that the growth of the food truck industry is causing local officials to make it easier to get the information necessary to be in compliance. Some cities already give food truck owners very clear guidelines on how to operate. Be sure to study the laws and regulations regarding food truck businesses in your area before venturing forward. We are working on a tool that will assist here, but the importance of accurate up to date information cannot be understated.

4. Competition

There is a vast competition in this industry. As the trend of the food truck business gains momentum, more and more people are interested in the idea. The critical way to overcome this challenge is to have an exceptional product, and an innovative brand. Creativity with marketing, and hard work to get your truck in high traffic areas as frequently as possible, will have you blowing past the competition quickly.

Chapter 2. Creating the Big Idea and The Team to Realize It

After you've weighed the pros and cons of owning a food truck business and decided to go with it, then you must first create the "big idea." Every successful business venture begins with a big idea that encompasses your vision and your mission. To come up with the plan, you must first determine what you are going to market. Great family recipes, and your own cooking discoveries can create a great foundation for your concept. Many food trucks use the creative fusion of a couple of different styles of food, combined in unexpected way to offer exciting new options to customers.

Another technique for making the "big idea" happen is to brainstorm and do some mind mapping. We recommend Simple Mind, which is an app to assist with mind mapping. Always carry around a notebook so that you can take note of all your thoughts. After brainstorming, then you can put your ideas together to create your plan. Inspiration can come from a great meal at a restaurant, or recipe book research online with a ton of free materials available at your fingertips.

A few examples to get your mind running on themes are as follows:

Barbeque – This is a relatively low cost food item that can be served quickly because it is largely prepared in advance, and it gives you a ton of options for creativity from using only locally sourced products, to fusion in food styles.

Out of region/regional cuisine – Food trucks often look to serve local favorites, and can be very successful in selling gumbo in New Orleans, or lobster rolls in Maine. But you know what often works better? Selling gumbo in Maine, and lobster rolls in New Orleans. Assuming you can source your food reasonably inexpensively, which is often as simple as forging relationships local to where the food is produced or harvested, you can offer fantastic fare to an audience that can't get it easily close by.

Waffles – seems simple enough but we have seen a ton of very successful waffle trucks. Whether they are offering chicken and waffles, traditional breakfast fare, or creative waffle sandwiches/pairings of another kind, these trucks do well because they are an attractive fun approach to getting a food truck fix.

Burgers – to mainstream? We have seen a peanut-butter jalepeno-cheddar-burger that would make you slap your granny it was so good. Be creative, but above all, use great fresh ingredients, and you will have an inexpensive food item you can sell for real profit.

Old World or Distant Fare – Some of the greatest inspiration for exceptional food trucks comes from a desire to celebrate family heritage and traditions. Does your grandmother have an incredible recipe for borsch? Maybe you grew up in a household that made its own bratwurst with sauerkraut. Incredible traditional recipes well prepared will launch a food truck business through the stratosphere. They offer an additional benefit of paring well with local fairs and festivals invitations to which you can secure easily.

Responsible/sustainable/locally produced fare – Food truck customers love feeling great about the healthy, safe, and even small town feel they get from supporting your local business' unique offerings that also come from local organic farms etc. Farm to table restaurants are very popular, and featuring local farmers, and food producers will help you to differentiate yourself while helping your local economy.

Dessert trucks – Great smells, or fantastic unusual sweets will drive folks from far around to your truck. These items often are prepped in advance, or have quick prep times, and they allow friends who may not be looking for a full meal to share something small that they can all enjoy.

The options are endless. Now go have some fun figuring this out!

We will discuss marketing later in the book, but your concept should be developed early on. Think about your branding, logos, and images that will draw people to the truck. If you are not artistic, there are a ton of local businesses that specialize in wraps that will cover the truck, and the artistic design of your brand. We recommend hiring a number of different illustrators from fiverr.com, who will put together logos and illustrations inexpensively, and can be used to form the inspiration for you truck.

Forming the Team

You may choose to be a sole proprietor business, but if you do that, you'll do everything on your own. If you decide to form a partnership, then you must pick the right partners. Poor decisions here will haunt you for the life of your business.

Screening for the Right Partners

Choosing a business partner or partners, for that matter, is like choosing a partner in life. You'll want to be with the person in the long run, and if it doesn't work out, then you are in for a lot of paperwork. With this in mind, it's best that you have criteria when choosing the right partners.

One of the most important things to consider when you choose a partner would be track record. Is your potential partner good at handling money? Does he or she have a history of integrity or are there a string of problems or disputes? Do not start a business with others simply because of money, potential connections, or experience. All of these are important, and can help you avoid common mistakes new business owners face, but you must be objective in selecting a partner, and if there is any hesitation, you should pass on inviting that person into your business. If that person is a friend or family, you must be even more careful, because you stand to lose more than the business if things don't work out.

Aside from integrity, experience, strengths, and record, another thing that your partner will need is a vision that is parallel to yours. What are the ultimate goals financially (i.e. we want to earn _____ in income), with respect to growth (i.e. we want 5 trucks, or to use this venue to create a brick and mortar restaurant), and what is the endgame (i.e. do we want to grow a business to sell it for a profit v.s. keeping it indefinitely as a primary source of income). All of this should be agreed at the outset. As mentioned earlier, a business partnership is very similar to a marriage in a sense that if the partners do not have a common goal, then critical problems will arise. Find someone whom you have good chemistry and synergy with and whom you can share your business' vision. On a final note, ownership percentages, and contributions of the parties to the business should be laid out and clearly understood from the start. Do not make the mistake of spending a ton of time or money, involving others, only to discover that you don't agree on these issues.

Each partner may have a different role. There will be partners who focus on investing money or assets, (these may or may not be interested in contributing time to the operations themselves), and there will be partners who focus on investing their expertise, (restaurant, cooking, or business experience for example.) When deciding on a partner, make sure that each offers at least one of these.

There are different of partners in a partnership with regard to contributions, but two kinds you should be aware of in setting up your business.

An active partner, also known as a managing partner, is the type of partner that actively participates in the management of the business. Managing partners could have also invested cash and assets into the business. Due to this, it is usually the active partners that have the biggest shares of profits.

A silent partner is also sometimes known as a sleeping or passive partner and is a partner that does not participate in the management of the business. They simply contribute capital. Their ownership share is based on their capital contributions they make, since they don't manage the business itself. A common challenge is that silent partners may have a nominal initial investment that gives them a material ownership share in the business. It is not uncommon for a truck to take off, earn well, and then resentment begins to build for those driving the business in being forced to share real profits with someone, who contributed an initial amount that seems small in comparison to the benefit they are realizing. This is why great care should be taken in giving up equity in the business for cash alone. If you don't absolutely need the money to get your truck off the ground, it is better to avoid purely silent partners.

Chapter 3. Drafting the Business Plan

After you and your partners have decided on what roles to play and how to split the profits, the next thing to do is to draft the business plan. This is the stage where the big idea will begin to take shape. We'll go over some of the important points that you'll need for your business plan, and then we'll take a look at an example of an actual business plan, but first, why do you need one?

Business plans are required if you are seeking third party capital from banks, the small business administration, or other lenders.

Even if you are not required to put one together to get such financing, the initial preparation and planning is critical to the success of your business, and will likely help you avoid costly mistakes.

If partners are involved the business plan is even more important to insure the alignment of vision necessary to avoid later disputes that can threaten the survival of the business.

Certain items unique to the food truck business should be included in your planning such as:

The Local Food Truck Marketplace

The Market Analysis portion of the business plan is one of the hardest to make since it takes a lot of objective data gathered from research of both primary and secondary sources.

In this case, we are interested in opening up a food truck business. Some industry research and statistics may be called for here, but the best research will be familiarizing yourself with local brands. This means internet research of the kinds of food trucks in your area (to help with differentiation and branding).

It also makes sense to look for "food truck lots." Many cities have parking lots that are leased, or used by a collection of trucks for the business lunch crowd. In many cases, food trucks are parked here permanently, and have a predictability that many food truck businesses lack. This may be the safest place to start your new business, because you will have documented foot traffic, predictable food costs, and relatively consistent sales, which are rare in the industry. The potential downside here is that your brand will need to be materially different than the offerings from the other trucks.

It also makes sense to do research on the annual local fairs, festivals, and events within 50 miles of your home base. This information is easy to find online, and organizers are often very happy to give you attendance, and exhibitor cost information, because they want you there. This information can help you project costs, and illustrate to potential investors where you plan to seek revenue in building your business.

Once you have worked through the local market, you will need to isolate the trucks that are either in direct or indirect competition with the truck you have conceived. Direct would be a substantially similar menu offering to the one you have in mind, and you would want to make sure that you are not setting yourself up to compete with an established brand in a narrow marketplace. Indirect competition would be some overlap in the menu, but sufficient difference in offerings that clients would conceivably be attracted to both businesses independently, were they to be at the same venue. Adjusting your own menu may be a way to reduce concerns that arise from direct and indirect competition.

Differentiation in brand and in product offering is critical to food truck success, and should be a huge part of your business plan. This doesn't mean you shouldn't start a food truck that is similar to another in the area, but it does mean that you should do so only after working out how you plan to compete with that truck. The strategy for success however is often more complicated than that.

Will you offer better quality food, a larger menu, longer service hours, or a better price? Perhaps some combination of these?

In planning business strategy, there are four basic business approaches that you can use in order to increase the likelihood of success for your business. These are cost leadership, differentiation, location, and hybrid.

Cost Leadership Strategy

This is very often the first strategy a new business seeks, and it can be a devastatingly bad one. Frankly, it should only be considered in a rare set of circumstances. Specifically this should only be considered for a very generic food offering in a high traffic environment. For example, if you are selling hot dogs, hamburgers, or fries at a state fair, and can move tremendous volume, reasonable profit is still possible. To compete with this strategy, extra research is required to get the lowest possible food cost at a quality you can live with. Do not think that you will build a repeat following simply by being cheap. In fact, if not careful, you may send the message that your food is lower quality or less desirable in an effort to attract clients with low cost.

Differentiation Strategy

The next strategy, and one which much more often makes sense is differentiation. As the name implies, the differentiation strategy would position your food truck in such a way that only you sell unique food products. Whether they are secret family recipes, hard to find food products, or creative dishes, these products set you apart because they cannot be offered by others. Quality is critical in the differentiation strategy, but if the food is great, and hard to find, your brand can achieve margins which are much more generous, leading to higher profit with lower sales and effort. This not only impacts the overall value of your business, it means a higher return on investment across the board.

Location Strategy

This can be a very effective strategy, especially at the start of the food truck for insuring a solid, even loyal customer base. An example of this can be found with a truck owner we know in Los Angeles. He learned that a local clothing manufacturer had hundreds of employees, many of whom did not drive cars. He asked the owner of the company if he could serve breakfast and lunch to those employees, and remit a small percentage of profits to the company for the right to set up there. The truck took off, and is now permanently located there, with another truck purchased in a matter of a few months to grow the business. If you are aware of an area that is underserved by local restaurants, or loaded with employees who cannot conveniently leave for lunch, this strategy can be very effective.

Hybrid Strategy

This strategy uses some combination of the above approaches to maximize the success of the truck. For example, we know of trucks that are in a particular place every Monday, and another on Tuesday etc. The scarcity created for customers who know if they want that item for lunch, they have to get it on a certain day can increase brand loyalty. This approach would combine both location and differentiation, while getting the extra benefit of spreading awareness of the brand. Others might have a different menu offering for festivals, or particularly high traffic events to take advantage of cost leverage strategy, while maintaining differentiation through a select offering of exclusive popular dishes.

Food Pricing

One of the hardest, and perhaps most important parts of putting together a business plan is to decide on the pricing of the product. In the case of food trucks, there are methods and strategies on how to properly price your dishes so that they can appeal to your target market and also get to a good profit. Pricing should be based on the cost of the raw materials that were used to make the dish.

Typically, most food establishments would set their pricing at between 35 to 45 percent markup of the dish's cost, which would include the food, and the plate, fork, garnishes etc. So, let's say that you are serving a dish with ingredients that reach up to a total of $5. You may make it have a selling price of $7.25. You can experiment with price, and exclusivity can drive costs up. For example, baseball stadiums can often charge $6 dollars for a $2 hot dog, because they have exclusivity. Your lunch crowd weekday guests are going to be much more sensitive to price than attendees at a festival, where there is an expectation that prices will be higher on food. If you price your items too inexpensively, you may quickly learn that the message you send customers is that the food isn't very good. Experiment, and you will find a comfortable range for each menu item.

If you are surrounded by other trucks, take the time to walk the grounds and get a sense of their offerings and prices. You don't want to charge $4 for a bottle of water, when all others are charging $2.

Another important consideration in pricing your items is labor, both in preparation in the kitchen and at the time of service from the truck. If a particular item is more labor intensive than others on your menu, you may reasonably adjust price to reflect that. Failure to take that into consideration can lead to a lack of profits that demotivates the owner, and sabotages the chances of success for the truck.

Use of Strategic Partnerships

Strategic partnerships should also be considered in the planning of the business. There is an exceptionally successful lobster roll brand that relies on a family fishing connection to provide inexpensive product, that can be marked up for a very nice margin. This is an example of a supplier strategic partnership that can provide a competitive advantage, which makes the business more attractive to financing, and improves chances of success. Other examples of strategic partnerships might be favorable lease rates, or exclusivity offered by a business owner, or festival organizer, with whom you share a small piece of the profit. It is worth your time to consider who you know, and how to leverage those relationships for competitive advantage.

Similarly, even if you don't have a supplier connection, you should spend a substantial amount of time interviewing and sampling food vendors to negotiate price, insure product quality, and keep your hard costs as low as possible. Your efforts in doing so should be documented in your business plan, to show those who may invest your preparation of succeeding in the business.

As you become more established, and work with various events, it is a good idea to keep up the relationships you had with organizers of previous events that you went to. Many are in this business, and can give you advanced notice, and great opportunities for good locations and events, as they are in the business.

It also really pays to have partners who are in media. Whether you donate to a cause that will be celebrated by the media, or offer a strange food offering that is newsworthy, this kind of attention can make your brand explode. Many food trucks offer food challenges such as an 8 pound burrito that is free if it can be finished by two eaters in less than an hour. Not much exposure from a cost standpoint, but an interesting story, and often news outlets love these angles for human interest to mix into gaps in slow news days.

Planning for Food Quantities

When pricing your food and beverages, you should take into consideration reasonable and expected serving sizes. It is your prerogative to offer large portions for value, or to draw guests, but you should at least start with normal portion sizes for purposes of calculations. If you plan to do 20% larger items, increase your cost by .2 etc.

Some food trucks also offer alcoholic beverages, beer, and/or wine. Be sure to check local requirements to make sure all necessary licenses are in place, but we have included a projection tool at the end of this book to assist with quantity planning.

Sample Business Plan Template

For those who are not familiar with making a business plan, here is a sample template that you can use for your food truck business.

    I. Executive Summary (This section would summarize what you are trying to achieve, a high level view of your brand, and how you plan to run the business. This would include an overview of what your business is all about)

    II. Objectives (This section would state the primary and secondary objectives of your business. Here, you will explain what exactly you want to achieve for both the long term and the short term)

III. Mission and Vision (This part would state your business' mission and vision as well as the business values in order to show investors your approach – could include valuing freshness, sustainable foods, and or support for a local charity or cause near to the founders)

IV. Company Summary (This will discuss more on the information regarding the company. It would include the owners of the business, as well as their profit share, the startup expenses that are needed for the business, the location of the kitchen or commissary, and the food truck locations)

1. Ownership

2. Overhead Startup Expenses

3. Kitchen Location

4. Food Truck Locations

    V. Products and Services (This part of the business plan will go into a detailed outline of the menu that you will serve to your customers. You also need to give a detailed list of the ingredients that you will use to make the food that you are serving on your menu, with food costs and projected sales pricing.

1.   Menu Description

2.   Raw Materials Sourcing

3.   Sales Literature

VI. Market Analysis Summary (The market analysis portion delves into studying and researching your market so that you will know how to make your moves to ride along the market and your targeted segment. This section was already explained above.)

1.   Industry Analysis
2.   Competition Analysis
3.   Market Trends Analysis

VII. Business Strategy (The business strategy portion would aid in creating your actual strategy for the food truck business so that you will know how to determine your competitive edge, important relationships, how to position your brand in the market, how to price your products, how to sell them, and who to partner up with. This section has been explained above)

1. Competitive Edge

2. Brand Positioning

3. Pricing Strategy

4. Strategic Partnerships

VIII.   Marketing Strategy (The marketing strategy would cover the mediums which can be used to further promote the product. The two types of marketing that may be used are the traditional marketing mediums like TV or print and the digital marketing mediums which consist of social media and internet related mediums)

1.   Traditional Marketing Media

2.   Digital Marketing Medium

IX.   Management Summary (The management summary would give an overview as to who are working in the management. The organizational structure is used to showcase who is in charge of what and corporate structure. This section would also look into the type of personnel and job openings there are so that the management will know who may be hired for the job)

1.   Management Team

2.   Organizational Structure

3.   Personnel to Hire

X.   Financial Plan (This section will go into the figures of the business meaning the finance and the numbers. This section will first cover how to get the breakeven point of your business, when you are starting up. This consists of the expenses, as well as potential income that you may have for the year. This can be shown in the profit forecast along with the other expenses and the breakeven analysis)

1.   Break Even Analysis

2.   Profit Forecast

- A note on getting financing: If your credit is bad to mediocre, expect to need a cosigner, large cash down payment (as a percentage of total cost), or be willing to put up viable collateral such as a home or car. Be sure you understand these risks. The better your credit, the lower the lender's expectations on down payments, cosigners and collateral. If possible seek out competing lenders to try to get the most favorable terms. A strong business plan can make a real difference in the answer you get from the bank.

Chapter 4. Before You Start the Business

Testing the Market

In business, you must always test the market to see what will work. After you have done your market research and have decided on the elements of your food truck, you now have to decide what you are going to serve and how much you are going to charge clients (based on the complete market analysis that you have done for your business plan).

When you have already decided what you will offer, dive into t he details. Let's start with the menu that you want to present. You must finalize the food that you are going to put in the menu. A very common mistake for food trucks is to have a menu that is more extensive than it needs to be, or that offers too diverse a selection. A large menu overwhelms guests, slows down ordering and processing times, and takes critical space in your truck for storage that could be used for your best sellers.

It is a good to have professionally designed menu boards that fit your brand, and if your truck is wrapped or decorated to draw attention from diners, your menu should look and feel consistent with that work. If your budget does not allow this kind of branding on the truck itself, a chalk board with very legible offerings works fine. In the beginning this will give you the flexibility to alter your offerings based on actual sales, before a more permanent decision has been made.

Testing the market is a very important step in opening up your food truck business because you want to know what is likely to work before you actually go in and invest your time, money and effort. There are a number of ways to test the market for your food:

1.   Research on the Success of Food Trucks Like Yours

The very first thing that you should do would be to research on food similar to the one you're making. If you see that their food is popular, you can bet that your food will also be popular as well if you make it taste great. The only challenge here would be how to market your brand and how to establish a name that distinguishes you sufficiently to avoid market confusion. This should likely have been done before reaching the test market phase.

2.   Try a Formal or Informal Survey

Another method of testing the market would be to create surveys. We love the taste plate approach, where you invite friends and relatives to a party or gathering, and offer your proposed menu for their feedback. It is important that these be guests that you absolutely trust to give you candid feedback. You really need to know if your items are too salty, or not spicy enough. This informal survey is very valuable to finalizing your menu. The exercise of making this food also gives you a feel for labor and prep time, which will help you decide if it makes sense to offer a particular item at a certain price. With the internet, this is now extremely easy to do formal surveys, because you can make use of survey apps or programs like Survey Monkey or even Google Forms. You have to just decide on the number of respondents that you would like to have for your survey and their demographic (your target market). From there, you can send out your survey and adjust your decisions on the results. If the results show that people like your idea, you may not need to make changes.

3.   "Dry" Runs

Before you spend a ton of money on a food truck, you should rent the truck you are proposing to buy, whether it is new or used, ask for a tester that will allow you to actually serve your food in real time. A poorly located fryer, or fridge that is too small will be very hard to adjust once you have paid the asking price. You may want a different truck. Similarly, if the plan is to staff the truck with one or more additional employees, you need to get in the truck with them, and see how you move together, to make decisions about who will perform what functions, when the truck is in operations. Finally, this gives you a chance at a festival, event, or with a prospective lunch crowd to see if your food actually sells, and how much. It would never make sense to attack this business and spend the capital required for success without having tried these things.

Creating the Brand

Your brand to be effective must accomplish all of the following:

- It makes your business easily recognizable. The easier your business is to recognize, the more people will associate your business with a certain product or service. This in turn translates into more sales.

- It must be pleasing, fun, and a positive reflection on your offering. If you are all organic, or locally sourced, your brand should reflect what makes you better.

- The brand should be professional, and consistent with your product. Some brands do well with characters, or funny animation, a gourmet brand offering more expensive or exclusive fair, should be more serious. This is critical to avoiding customer confusion

- Your brand should be highly visible, from the truck or otherwise, and unique to you, so that customers can see it and instantly recognize what you offer.

- Your brand is much more than a logo, or wrap on the truck, it is a feel you are trying to share with the customer that draws them to your business. Logo is important, but all of your branded items, should be consistent with each other, and contribute to a greater understanding of your business and offerings.

- All of the best brands are easy to remember and simple in design. The very best brands are the ones that you don't need to explain. Once a person sees the brand, he or she will immediately know what your food truck is all about.

- The best brands also hold an emotional appeal to the target market. The emotional connection that you will make will depend on the demographic and psychographic profile of the target market. In other words, you have to know what makes them "tick". You have to know what strikes their emotional strings and work your brand identity on that.

- Lastly, your brand identity should be consistent. If you have multiple trucks, they should be similarly decked out with signage or wraps.

Examples of Cool Food Truck Brands

Just to give an idea, here are a few very well-known examples of food truck brands that made it pretty big in America.

In Boston, there's a food truck known as Roxy's Grilled Cheese which is very known for serving delicious grilled cheese sandwiches. They have a lot of different types of sandwiches with everything from guacamole to Applewood bacon. Of course, you can enjoy having a simple glorious grilled cheese with them as well.

If you are into slider burgers, Easy Slider in Dallas is the place to go to. For those who don't know what sliders are, they are small bite sized burgers. Sliders became quite a fad a while before the food truck industry took off. When the food truck industry took off, slider burgers also followed. Easy Slider sells nothing but delicious slider burgers with Angus beef patties and many different kinds of other ingredients and spreads. These are simple, easy to share fun foods.

Another noteworthy food truck brand is Natedogs which can be found in Minneapolis. They sell classic hot dogs in buns with a twist. Their hot dogs have unique dressings like beer mustard, relish, and caramelized onions.

Exotic cuisine can be found in a food truck known as Quiero Arepas in Denver. The menu is inspired by the cuisine of Venezuela. They serve burrito dishes with shredded beef, mozzarella cheese, and black beans. Their wraps also have many different varieties of stuffing that can be mixed and matched to suit the tastes of the buyers.

Chapter 5 Financial Planning

A very crucial part of the business plan would be the breakeven analysis as well as the profit forecast. These two calculations will give you an insight on how you must run your business in the first few months of operations, and give comfort to financers as to your ability to repay the debt. While we are on that subject, don't try to convince a financer to loan you money on a truck that is in poor condition. Either find something new, or in excellent condition, or get a quote to put the truck in top condition. Do not expect a bank or finance company to lend its money on a bad truck, and don't even think about doing that yourself. This is not a place to shortcut.

Let's take a look at how to compute for the breakeven points first.

BEP or breakeven point, in the context of a food truck operation should be thought of in terms of:

P which symbolizes the price of each dish; (we have included a pricing tool, which we can send electronically upon request to products@newbizplaybook.com)

X which symbolizes the number of units per dish served;

V which symbolizes the variable cost per unit. Variable costs consists of costs that contribute directly to the forming of each unit of products (e.g. ingredients to make the food, gas used for cooking). Variable costs are not standard and vary depending on the usage.

FC symbolizes the fixed costs that are incurred per month. Fixed costs are standard costs that you have to pay whether or not you make any money or not. Fixed costs are standard per month (e.g. electricity bill, phone bill, web server costs).

Now that we have the variables defined, let's talk about how to use them in a formula to solve for breakeven points.

First, you can look for the BEP in units so you know how much food you should sell to reach our breakeven point for the first year of operations. The BEP in units can be solved like this:

BEP X = FC/V-P

This is X (number of units to BEP) is equal to FC (fixed costs) divided by V (variable costs) minus P (unit price per dish).

Once you have the BEP number of units, you can now determine your BEP price. You simply multiply price per unit and the BEP number of units to get your BEP price.

It is formulated as follows:
BEP Price = X (BEP X)

Now, this formulation is just assuming that you have one product in your store. However, since you have a food truck, you will most likely have a lot of dishes on your menu (including drinks and add-ons).

With this in mind, the more appropriate formulation to use would be to get the weighted averages for selling price and variable costs. After you get these two, you can plot them into your formula.

In order to get the weighted average, you can use this formula:
(Selling price of product 1 × Sales percentage of product 1) + (Selling price of product 2 × Sales percentage of product 2) + (Selling price of product 3 × Sales percentage of product 3) + (Selling price of product 4 × Sales percentage of product 4)........

In order to get the Sales percentage of product, you have to decide on a ranking of the products to determine which will sell the most to which would sell the least. The total percentage of all the products will equal 100%, so you have to split the 100% to all these products.

Once you've computed the weighted average of all your dishes, then you also compute for the weighted average for variable costs as shown below:

(Variable expenses of product 1 × Sales percentage of product 1) +

(Variable expenses of product 2 × Variable expenses of product 2) +

(Variable expenses of product 3 × Sales percentage of product 3) +

(Variable expenses of product 4 × Sales percentage of product 4).........

After getting your weighted averages for variable costs and the selling prices, you can plot them into this formula:

BEP X = FC/ Weighted Average V - Weighted Average P

To better understand how to do this, we'll make use of a case scenario as an example.

Let's say you want to open up a burger food truck called Billy's Burger Stop wherein you will sell different kinds of burgers along some fries and drinks.

At the start of the business, Billy's wants to introduce 3 burgers, 1 kind of fries, and lemonade.

Billy's will be selling Angus Burgers at $8,
Veggie Burgers at $7,
and Bacon Burgers at $8.

Billy's would also be selling fries at $4
And lemonade at $2.

Variable expenses would include $3 for Angus Burger,
$2.5 for Veggie Burgers,
$3 for Bacon Burgers,
fries at $1.50
and lemonade at 50c.

Billy's decided that the Angus Burger will have an SPP (sales percentage of product) of 30%,

Veggie Burgers 20%,

Bacon Burgers 20%,

fries at 10%

and lemonade at 20%.

To compute for the breakeven point, first we compute for the weighted average of the selling price.

This would be (8x30%) + (7x20%) + (8x20%) + (4x10%) + (2x20%)= 5.6

After that, you get the weighted average of the variable cost which would be:
(3x30%) + (2.5x20%) + (3x20%) + (1.5x10%) + (0.5x20%)= 2.25

From there, we can plot the figures into the formula. Let's pack the FC at around $4,000 for everything including kitchen expenses, gas, rental etc.

This will be 4,000/5.6-2.25 = 1045 units. This means that your truck would have to sell approximately 1,045 units to break even.

We have included a cash flow tool below. Email us for a customizable electronic version.

Creating the Profit Forecast

After you know how to compute for the Break Even Point, you can now go ahead and make your profit forecast. Your profit forecast is very important because it will help you determine what month you can reach breakeven and when you will start profiting. You will also see all of your expenses to know how to do some pencil pushing. Let's get started with the expenses.

Compiling All Expenses

Before you create the profit forecast, you must first list down all of your expenses. When you start your food truck business, you must think first about your overhead expenses which are the expenses that that you use to get the business going. These would include the cost to get the truck, the advertising wrap for the truck, and the first food inventory for the first six months. We have included a list of respected truck builders and sellers from locations all over the country to help you project costs, and a food cost projection tool, that allows for accurate planning on a per dish basis.

For your truck, you may choose to either rent or buy one. If you are renting a food truck, you will be paying a monthly fee for the usage while if you buy one, you will just pay everything outright, unless you get a note on the vehicle.

Be sure to think about would be the kitchen expenses, particularly extra equipment that must be purchased or rent if using a prep kitchen.

You must also think about designing your truck and your truck advertising. Aside from that, you must already take into consideration the labor that you will use for your truck. Assistants and cooks may be needed depending on how big you want your business to be at the start.

If you plan to start lean, you may just have 2 or 3 prep and cooking staff.

Lastly, you must source for your ingredients and add that as expenses. These are the major expenses you have to think of.

Monthly Expense Forecasting Tool

	Month 1		
	Price	Quantity	Total Sales in Dollars
Unit Price	xxx	xxx	$ xxx
Less: Cost of Sales	xxx	xxx	xxx
Profit per Piece	xxx		xxx
Security Deposit and Advanced Rental Expense			xxx
Truck Purchase/Rent			xxx
Kitchen Purchase/Rent			xxx
Marketing Expenses			xxx
Business License and Registration			xxx
Utilities Expenses			xxx
Salaries Expenses			xxx
Truck Design Expense			xxx
Miscellaneous Expense			xxx
Insurance			xxx
Total Expenses			XXX
Net Income/Loss			xxx

This forecasting table was designed to project costs on a per month basis.

It contains the price, the quantity, and total price in dollars. The price heading would determine the unit price, and the quantity heading would determine the estimated quantity that you can sell in the first month. The unit price multiplied by the estimated quantity will equal to total sales in dollars.

You will also have the unit price row heading along with cost of sales. In order to get the profit per piece, you have to subtract the cost of sales from the unit price. Under the total sales in dollars column heading, you will get the total gross profit for the month.

Right below that, is the list of expenses. The list of expenses are to be totaled in order to get the total expenses for the month. From there we subtract the total expenses to the total profit and we get the net income/net loss for the month. If the total profit exceeds total expenses, we have a net income, if it doesn't, then we have a net loss.

It is also through this table that you can determine how long it will take for you to reach your breakeven point. Take note that this tool doesn't assume any additional or prior capital infusion.

Determining Capital Requirement

By determining the income forecast, you now can determine the required capital infusion for the business. Most people are conservative and would infuse capital to cover the first three to six months of expenses whether or not the business reaches the breakeven point or not, and count on the sales to increase. This gives you a window to make mistakes, learn what your real sales are, and what items on your menu are driving business. It certainly makes sense to revisit financial projections, breakeven, and profit/loss analysis every 30 days or so in the beginning to avoid purchasing food that you won't use, or incurring unnecessary expenses.

Complete the projection tool above, and plan for the number of months you will cover regardless of sales, and base your capital requirement on the number reached by computing the total expenses for a period of time plus the cost of sales for the said period of time.

If you are borrowing capital to start the business, consider negotiating a delay in the first payment on the note for 90-120 days to allow you to reinvest in the business, so there is sufficient capital in the business for operations.

Chapter 6. Operations

Covering All the Legalities

Spend the time up front to research all required licenses and certifications needed before you can begin operations. Every city in the country is different, and the last thing you want to do is spend money, and incur debt that you have an obligation to repay, only to discovery you cannot even start your business.

Licenses

Tax – You will need an EIN or employer identification number. If you are operating as a sole proprietor this can be your social security number. Depending upon the state in which you operate, there may also be sales or franchise permits needed to make sure you are in compliance.

State Permits – Your state may have particular health or operations permits that are required to start your business. We highly recommend the SBA licenses and permits website for details. See **https://www.sba.gov/starting-business/business-licenses-permits/state-licenses-permits**

Local Permits – Your city may also have requirements for permits on health, signage, zoning, taxes, or alarms. We recommend the above referenced links, as well as the official city website for your town for specifics.

Incorporation

If you are operating as a sole proprietor, you can be personally liable for things like work related injuries, food poisoning, or a collision. We recommend that you get counsel about the possibility of forming a corporation or LLC, which can help you intelligently protect personal assets from business exposure. Many states have the required formation forms on their secretary of state websites for free download.

Employer Requirements

Before you can hire employees, you will need to insure that they are eligible to legally work in your area. In the United States employers must complete I-9's which prove work eligibility, and W-4's which determine income tax withholding. For further information, the IRS publishes a tax guide for employers at **https://www.irs.gov/pub/irs-pdf/p15.pdf**

The SBA also has easy to understand information at **https://www.sba.gov/managing-business/running-business/managing-business-finances-accounting/10-steps-setting-payroll-system**

You may also be required as an employer to display certain posters for employees. This information can be found at: **http://webapps.dol.gov/elaws/posters.htm**

Insurance

You will want to consult a qualified insurance professional to discuss workers compensation, unemployment insurance, and auto/general liability coverages for your business.

Planning for the Operations

Marketing

We've also discussed marketing expenses in the income forecasting portion of the book, but we'll delve into the details here.

The primary medium of marketing or advertising your food truck business would be your food truck itself. Your food truck is already considered a moving advertisement. A professional well designed wrap can make a huge difference in the profitability of your truck. Do not cut corners here.

Social Media and Digital Marketing

Loyal customers will want to know where you are, and how to find you. Social media can be a huge way to bring customers to your truck. Set up a facebook page and let your followers know where you are, what your special items are for the day, or what you are celebrating at your truck. Post pictures of your fantastic food, and customers enjoying it. When people have a great experience, they will want to share. Consider tools like buffer and hootsuite to manage and schedule posts throughout the day, so you don't have to interrupt your food service.

Additionally Apps such as Truckily and Nom Nom Finder are great for sharing your food truck's location, updates, and opening hours. This way, those who want to look for you can just go to you any time they want.

A webpage is a great place to post reviews, your truck's travel schedule, menu items, and coupons or incentives that will draw more customers to your truck. The page doesn't have to be large or complicated, but it should definitely match your brand. Another great use of marketing on the webpage can be digital forms for scheduling catering, or special events that allow your customers to book your truck for their events or parties. To keep costs low, consider sites such as elance.com, or odesk for competitive bids.

Other social media platforms such as Twitter, Instagram, Pinterest etc. can help draw traffic to your truck and build name and brand recognition.

It also makes sense to consider creating an email community that you can use to publicize where you will be, and what is happening with your business. There are a number of tools to help with this, and we would recommend mailchimp and optinskin for your consideration.

Events Marketing

As mentioned earlier, you can gain more sales through events marketing or promoting your food truck in events. For example, festivals and carnivals are great places to earn real money. Lots of people will be gathered in one place to celebrate, so everyone is in a festive and buying mood. Because of this, your food truck will definitely make a lot of money here. The trick in knowing when festivals are would be to make use of the internet. Research on local festivals in your area like a hot-air balloon festival or a food festival.

Client Interaction

Your client interaction is a critical form of marketing, and enhancing the guest experience. You must have killer customer service, and connect with customers in a way that makes your truck feel like community.

Back-end Operations

Marketing is one of the most important aspects of your food truck business, but if you don't have an efficient backend to support the customers that you brought in, your food truck won't be successful anyway. There are three things that you have to really take into consideration when you prepare for your back-end operations. These are the off truck kitchens and commissaries, inventory and maintenance system, and the manpower and personnel. Let's start with the kitchens and commissaries.

Off Truck Kitchens and Commissaries

As mentioned in the earlier parts of the book, you will be needing a kitchen where you can prepare your food and stock up on your inventory.

One of the most common reasons for hiring or renting a commissary is storage of food and equipment. Today, commissaries are modeled after supermarkets, so that the customers have an easier time accessing the food, and refrigerators, ovens, etc., can be configured to the needs of a particular tenant. These benefits are nice, but costs are a material concern with commissaries. If you are running multiple trucks, it will be difficult to handle food prep and storage out of a private kitchen. Some food truckers build a second kitchen in their garages, and do it that way. The space is deductible as a business expense, and allows for the separation of personal food and equipment from commercial items.

Some cities do not allow you to use your private kitchen as a storehouse because of health code limitations. Be sure to check this out as you do cost projections, because that kind of extra cost can be enough to stifle profits.

Inventory and Maintenance

Food trucks need to keep inventory of food, plates, spices, bags and any other items that may wear out or be delivered to customers during the course of the day. If you are using a fryer, that oil can be cleaned, but will have to be replaced with some frequency.

The best inventory systems monitor sales, and adjust your food and equipment stores accordingly. They cost more, but the automation can save significant labor in doing food and equipment counts after every shift. These systems will also alert you to food waste, and/or deviation in portion amounts where there is a mismatch. This is important in keeping food costs manageable.

If you have sufficient storage, buying in bulk will give you a lower food cost, and reduce the time, effort, and cost of multiple trips to reload.

As for maintenance, you must make sure that you regularly maintain your truck, and the kitchen equipment/generators to keep things running properly. It pays to add a maintenance expense to your fixed costs so that your truck will last long and can serve more. It is advisable to make a regular schedule for maintenance so that you can monitor the cost of your truck maintenance.

Managing Operations

We have attached a tool below to assist with managing operations and costs for your food truck.

Food Preparation and Procedure

Training employees to be able to prepare quality products consistently every time is critical to your business. We recommend that employees cook with full supervision for at least a week before being "certified" to prepare those items on their own.

You also want to have a very simple system for conveying recipe information, so that employees can get the specific ingredients and amounts quickly. We recommend the template card we have attached, and suggest that each menu item have a laminated card such as the one featured in the template to insure that they are easy to read and use in a food preparation environment.

Labor and Personnel

For a food truck business, you don't really need many employees, especially if you are starting out small. Typically, a food truck business will consist of a driver, two assistants in the truck (these assistants can cook, prepare food, tend the cashier, and do inventory), and another assistant in the kitchen who will look after the back-end and prepare the food. You can reduce these costs by handling prep yourself, or including yourself as one of the staff during operations.

When done properly, the food truck business requires the owner to be very hands on to make sure everything is done properly.

We have attached an employee timecard template, and you can email us for a customizable version

Planning for Long Term Growth

After you've been in business for some time and have gotten a solid client base, you might think it is now time to grow the business. You and your partners should discuss the expected growth of the brand, and the form it will take at the time of the startup.

Does growth mean more trucks? Are you trying to open a brick and mortar restaurant? What are the goals for timing of debt payoff to insure that the business has the protection it needs, while still responsibly paying investors? Is a franchise system an option?

There are numerous ways to profit from your successful brand, but none of them should be seriously considered until you have been in operation for at least a year, unless immediate demand will exceed expenses dramatically. There are a couple of reasons for this. As the owner, you need to know if the success of the truck is based on seasonal traffic, or circumstances, such that you have very busy months and very slow ones. Second, you need to give the business a chance to mature with all of the mistakes, issues, and problems that might have been unforeseeable at the beginning, so that you can plan for those issues at the time of expansion. Finally, premature expansion can create a capital shortage that threatens an otherwise healthy business. Be smart here.

Document Management

As your business grows, your need to keep and maintain documents will grow with it. We highly recommend having a fireproof lock box for key documents that do not have to be displayed on the truck itself.

You should take digital photos of all licenses and permits in case one is damaged, so you have proof of compliance while you get your replacement.

Supplies

Planning supplies is also going to be part of your operations cost, and you do not want to be in the field only to discovery that you do not have everything you need to run your business.

A short list of things to check for would include:

All cooking and prep tools
Pots, Pans, Cutting/Prep boards
Napkins
To go containers and customer plates
Bags
Straws
Cups and lids of soda fountain is used
Dish soap
Paper towels
Gloves
Trash bags
Floor mats
Glass and stainless steel cleaner
Degreaser

Recipe Costing Template

			COST DISTRIBUTION
DATE	2/9/2017		
DISH NAME	salmon		
EST. SALE PPRICE	$	27.35	
TOTAL COST	$	7.05	
COST MARGIN	%	25.77	
NET PROFIT	$	20.30	

Cost distribution pie chart: 33%, 67%, 0%

PRIMARY INGREDIENTS

Product Name	Qty.	Cost (per unit)		Total Cost	
Salmon	1	$	4.70	$	4.70
TOTAL				$	4.70

SECONDARY INGREDIENTS

Product Name	Qty Gm	Cost Kg/Lt		Total Cost	
Potato	1	$	10.00	$	0.01
Tartar Sauce	0.5	$	3.50	$	0.00
Green Beans	1.5	$	4.40	$	0.01
TOTAL				$	0.02

UTILITY AND PREP. COST

Name	Total Cost	
Preparation	$	2.00
Gas	$	0.12
Electricity	$	0.11
Water	$	0.10
TOTAL	$	2.33

Insert a Photo of the Dish

PREPARATION

ALLERGIES

Prepared By	Approved By
Occupation	Occupation

Food Truck Startup Spreadsheet

Equipment	Estimated Cost	Notes
This will be cost for the vehicle, any external decorations or wrap, and the interior restaurant equipment such as grills, refrigerators, food storage and cabinets etc. We recommend as much stainless steel as you can afford. We have a tool herein with some vendors	$30,000 - $80,000	You can find less expensive trucks that are used, or that have less features, but if you are buying a used truck, have a mechanic inspect thoroughly
Initial Product Inventory - food and beverages	$1,000 - $2,000	
Permits and Licenses	$100 - $500	Different cities have vary, and some may require that you take sanitation, or food service classes to get certified by the city
Website	Free - $2,500	Your most important marketing other than word of mouth. Don't get cheap here.
Cash Register/point of sale for credit cards	$200 - $1,000	Phones and tablets using square or other credit transaction apps will be helpful in the beginning
Uniforms / T-Shirts	$0 - $1,000	Part of your branding
Paper Products (Cups/Plates / Napkins, etc.)	$200 - $300	
Misc. Expenses (Like a Chalk Menu)	$500 - $2000	Plan for some unexpected expenses here and put it into the budget.
Smallwares: Pots, Pans, etc.	$1000 - $2000	
Fire Extinguisher	$100 - $300	
Total Low End	$33,300	
Total High End	$91,600	

Food Truck Operations Spreadsheet

Item	Monthly Estimated Cost	Notes
Parking or Host Charges	varies	You may have to pay for a stall, or pay a business a percentage of revenue to offer products to their employees
Phone / Internet	$100 - $200	
Fuel	$500	This will vary a lot.
Labor	8-15 dollars per hour	$8 - $15 per hour is average rate.
Repairs	$1,000	Just for protection
Food / Beverage Restock	varies based upon sales expect to replenish food stocks weekly, obviously if you have a great weekend, it may happen more often	
Paper Product Restock	$800-$1600	Depends on food cost and frequency of operation.
Insurance	$50 - $150	Depends on food cost and frequency of operation.
Total:		

Great Sites for Purchasing Food Trucks

http://www.buyfoodtruck.net/

http://www.cateringtruck.com/

http://apexspecialtyvehicles.com/

http://www.onthemovetrucks.com/otm-food-trucks

http://www.mr-trailers.com/

http://www.customconcessionsusa.com/

http://www.detroitcustomcoach.com/

https://northwestmobilekitchens.com/

http://www.bostonianbody.com/default.html

http://www.sybbq.com/

http://doublertrailers.com/

https://snoshack.com/

http://mobilekitchensolutions.net/contact-us/

Alcohol and Beverage Planning

Concerning drinks, let the following list guide you:

Soft drinks: One to two 8-ounce servings per person per hour.

Punch: One to two 4-ounce servings per person per hour.

Tea: One to two 8-ounce servings per person per hour.

Coffee: One to two 4-ounce servings per person per hour.

Water: Always provide it. Two standard serving pitchers per table are usually enough.

Again, err on the side of having too much. If people are eating a lot and having fun, they tend to consume more liquid.

Alcohol Consumption and Pricing Projection Tool

There is always some subjectivity in alcohol planning. The assumption here is that 75% of the guests are drinking alcohol. This should be discussed, as a higher percentage of children in attendance, a group of heavier drinkers etc., could impact these assumptions.

As always we recommend adding 10% to all estimates. You will frustrate guests if there is insufficient alcohol, so make sure they are in agreement with your assumptions on numbers. They will know their guests better than anyone. The cost estimates assume average costs on beer, wine, and liquor. Premium beer, wine, and liquor would also mean increased costs. This also assumes equal consumption i.e. 25% each of beer, wine, and liquor. Beer drinkers tend to range closer to 40%, but these figures make scaling for your needs much easier.

The following should help plan for reception alcohol consumption. BD = beer drinker, WD = wine drinker, LD = liquor drinker

	Small Wedding (100 guests)	
	Amount	Cost
Beer	5 cases per 25 BD	75.00
Wine	20 bottles per 25 WD	160.00
Liquor	6 750 ml bottles per 25 LD	90.00

	Medium Wedding (200 guests)	
	Amount	Cost
Beer	9 cases per 50 BD	135.00
Wine	40 bottles per 50 WD	320.00
Liquor	12 750 ml bottles per 50 LD	180.00

	Large Wedding (100)	
	Amount	Cost
Beer	3 Kegs 100 BD	270.00
Wine	79 bottles per 100 WD	632.00
Liquor	24 750 ml bottles per 100 LD	360.00

Appetizers

As you determine the appetizer quantity, consider what purpose the appetizers will serve. If you're serving appetizers before a main meal, you don't need as many as you do if the appetizers are the meal itself. Because appetizers are different from other food items, how much you need depends on several factors. Appetizers don't lend themselves to a quantity chart, per se, but let the following list guide you:

- For appetizers preceding a full meal, you should have at least four different types of appetizers and six to eight pieces (total) per person. For example, say you have 20 guests. In that case, you'd need at least 120 total appetizer pieces.

- For appetizers without a meal, you should have at least six different types of appetizers. You should also have 12 to 15 pieces (total) per person. For example, if you have 20 guests, you need at least 240 total appetizer pieces. This estimate is for a three-hour party. Longer parties require more appetizers.

- The more variety you have, the smaller portion size each type of appetizer will need to have. Therefore, you don't need to make as much of any one particular appetizer.

- When you serve appetizers to a crowd, always include bulk-type appetizers. Bulk-type foods are items that aren't individually made, such as dips or spreads. If you forgo the dips and spreads, you'll end up making hundreds of individual appetizer items, which may push you over the edge. To calculate bulk items, assume 1 ounce equals 1 piece.

- Always try to have extra items, such as black and green olives and nuts, for extra filler.

When appetizers precede the meal, you should serve dinner within an hour. If more than an hour will pass before the meal, then you need to increase the number of appetizers. Once again, always err on the side of having too much rather than too little.

Quantity planning for soups, sides, main courses, and desserts

The following tables can help you determine how much food you need for some typical soups, sides, main courses, and desserts. If the item you're serving isn't listed here, you can probably find an item in the same food group to guide you.

You may notice a bit of a discrepancy between the serving per person and the crowd servings. The per-person serving is based on a plated affair (where someone else has placed the food on the plates and the plates are served to the guests). In contrast, buffet-style affairs typically figure at a lower serving per person because buffets typically feature more side dish items than a plated meal does. Don't use the quantity tables as an exact science; use them to guide you and help you make decisions for your particular crowd. If you're serving a dish that you know everyone loves, then make more than the table suggests. If you have a dish that isn't as popular, you can get by with less.

Soups and Stews

Soup or Stew	Per Person	Crowd of 25	Crowd of 50
Served as a first course	1 cup	5 quarts	2-1/2 gallons
Served as an entree	1-1/2 to 2 cups	2 to 2-1/2 gallons	4 gallons

Main Courses

Entree	Per Person	Crowd of 25	Crowd of 50
Baby-back ribs, pork spareribs, beef short ribs	1 pound	25 pounds	50 pounds
Casserole	N/A	Two or three 9-x-13-inch casseroles	Four or five 9-x-13-inch casseroles
Chicken, turkey, or duck (boneless)	1/2 pound	13 pounds	25 pounds
Chicken or turkey (with bones)	3/4 to 1 pound	19 pounds	38 pounds
Chili, stew, stroganoff, and other chopped meats	5 to 6 ounces	8 pounds	15 pounds
Ground beef	1/2 pound	13 pounds	25 pounds
Maine lobster (about 2 lbs. each)	1	25	50
Oysters, clams, and mussels (medium to large)	6 to 10 pieces	100 to 160 pieces	200 to 260 pieces
Pasta	4 to 5 ounces	7 pounds	16 pounds
Pork	14 ounces	22 pounds	44 pounds
Roast (with bone)	14 to 16	22 to 25 pounds	47 to 50 pounds

ounces

	Per Person	Crowd of 25	Crowd of 50
Roast cuts (boneless)	1/2 pound	13 pounds	25 pounds
Shrimp (large: 16 to 20 per pound)	5 to 7 shrimp	7 pounds	14 pounds
Steak cuts (T-bone, porterhouse, rib-eye)	16 to 24 ounces	16 to 24 ounces per person	16 to 24 ounces per person
Turkey (whole)	1 pound	25 pounds	50 pounds

Side Dishes

Side Dish	Per Person	Crowd of 25	Crowd of 50
Asparagus, carrots, cauliflower, broccoli, green beans, corn kernels, peas, black-eyed peas, and so on	3 to 4 ounces	4 pounds	8 pounds
Corn on the cob (broken in halves when serving buffet-style)	1 ear	20 ears	45 ears
Pasta (cooked)	2 to 3 ounces	3-1/2 pounds	7 pounds
Potatoes and yams	1 (medium)	6 pounds	12 pounds
Rice and grains (cooked)	1-1/2 ounces	2-1/2 pounds	5 pounds

Side Salads

Ingredient	Per Person	Crowd of 25	Crowd of 50
Croutons (medium size)	N/A	2 cups	4 cups
Dressing (served on the side)	N/A	4 cups	8 cups
Fruit salad	N/A	3 quarts	6 quarts
Lettuce (iceberg or romaine)	N/A	4 heads	8 heads
Lettuce (butter or red leaf)	N/A	6 heads	12 heads
Potato or macaroni salad	N/A	8 pounds	16 pounds
Shredded cabbage for coleslaw	N/A	6 to 8 cups (about 1 large head of cabbage)	12 to 16 cups (about 2 large heads of cabbage)
Vegetables (such as tomato and cucumber)	N/A	3 cups	6 cups

Breads

Bread	Per Person	Crowd of 25	Crowd of 50
Croissants or muffins	1-1/2 per person	3-1/2 dozen	7 dozen
Dinner rolls	1-1/2 per person	3-1/2 dozen	7 dozen
French or Italian bread	N/A	Two 18-inch loaves	Four 18-inch loaves

Desserts

Dessert	Per Person	Crowd of 25	Crowd of 50
Brownies or bars	1 to 2 per person	2-1/2 to 3 dozen	5-1/2 to 6 dozen
Cheesecake	2-inch wedge	Two 9-inch cheesecakes	Four 9-inch cheesecakes
Cobbler	1 cup	Two 9-x-9-x-2-inch pans	Four 9-x-9-x-2-inch pans
Cookies	2 to 3	3 to 4 dozen	6 to 8 dozen
Ice cream or sorbet	8 ounces	1 gallon	2 gallons
Layered cake or angel food cake	1 slice	Two 8-inch cakes	Four 8-inch cakes
Pie	3-inch wedge	Two or three 9-inch pies	Four or five 9-inch pies
Pudding, trifles, custards, and the like	1 cup	1 gallon	2 gallons
Sheet cake	2-x-2-inch piece	1/4 sheet cake	1/2 sheet cake

Time Card Template
(for full customizable version email foodtruckpro to
products@newbizplaybook.com)

ACME FOOD TRUCK INC.

TIME CARD / PRODUCTION REPORT

		WK END	
JOB NAME			

DESCRIPTION	MON		TUES		WED		THURS		FRI	
	LF/SHEETS	HRS	LF/SHEETS	HRS	LF/SHEETS	HRS	LF/SHEETS	HRS	LF/SHEETS	HRS
TOTAL / FT/SHEETS										
TOTAL HRS		0	0	0	0	0	0	0	0	0

Weekly Cash Flow Template
(for full customizable version email foodtruckpro to
products@newbizplaybook.com)

	Mon	Tue	Wed	Thu	Fri	Sat	Sun	Weekly Subtotal
Sales Forecast								
Sales	3,000	3,000	3,000	3,000	3,000			15,000
AR (Daily)	2,400	2,400	2,400	2,400	2,400	0	0	12,000
Opening Balance		600	1,200	1,800	2,400	(3,000)	(3,000)	0
Revenue								
Cash & Credit Card Sales	600	600	600	600	600	0	0	3,000
A/R Collected (<30 days)	0	0	0	0	0	0	0	0
A/R Collected (30-60 days)	0	0	0	0	0	0	0	0
Loan From Bank								0
Loan From Owner								0
Loan From Owner								0
Other Expenses Repaid								0
Commisary								0
Revenue Totals	600	600	600	600	600	0	0	3,000
Expenses								
Owner's Salary	0	0	0	0	0	0	0	0
Owner's Salary	0	0	0	0	0	0	0	0
Rent (Office)	0	0	0	0	0	0	0	0
Salary (Staff)								0
Phones	0	0	0	0	0	0	0	0
Advertising								0
Leads	0	0	0	0	0	0	0	0
Lease Payments	0	0	0	0	0	0	0	0
Contingency	0	0	0	0	0	0	0	0
Loan repayment	0							0
Commission	0	0	0	0	6,000	0	0	6,000
Synergy (Inventory)	0	0	0	0	0	0	0	0
Shipping	0	0	0	0	0	0	0	0
Contractor Expenses	0							0
Bad Debt & Returns	0	0	0	0	0	0	0	0
Expenses Subtotal	0	0	0	0	6,000	0	0	6,000
Monthly Net Cash In / (Out)	600	600	600	600	(5,400)	0	0	(3,000)
Closing Balance	600	1,200	1,800	2,400	(3,000)	(3,000)	(3,000)	

Start-up Expenses	
Web Site	1500
Furniture	2500
Miscellaneous	1000
Phone System	1000
Rent first/last	4000
Loan (JD)	
Inventory	10,000
Total	20000
Loan	75000
Starting Cash Flow	55000

Food Inventory Template
(for full customizable version email foodtruckpro to
products@newbizplaybook.com)

Pack	Size	Unit	Desc	Unit Counted	Case $	Unit Price	Count	Extended
Dairy Products								
4	4.25LB	CS	Butter Chip Cntl 47 Ct Aa	cs	36.68	36.68	1	$36.68
36	1 LB	CS	Butter Solid Unslt Usda Aa	cs	67.09	67.09	2	$134.18
9	.5 GAL	CS	Buttermilk 1% Low Fat	cs	19.26	19.26	3	$57.78
				cs		0.00		$0.00
				cs		0.00		$0.00
				cs		0.00		$0.00
				cs		0.00		$0.00
				cs		0.00		$0.00
				cs		0.00		$0.00
				CS		0.00		$0.00
				CS		0.00		$0.00
				CS		0.00		$0.00
				CS		0.00		$0.00
				CS		0.00		$0.00
				CS		0.00		$0.00
				CS		0.00		$0.00
				CS		0.00		$0.00
				CS		0.00		$0.00
				CS		0.00		$0.00
				CS		0.00		$0.00
				CS		0.00		$0.00
				CS		0.00		$0.00
				CS		0.00		$0.00
Dairy Products Total								**$228.64**

Carrot Soup

Preparation time: 10 minutes	Cook time: 45 minutes	Serves: 6 to 8

Ingredients

- 4 tablespoons butter
- 2 medium onions, sliced
- 1 sprig thyme
- 2 1/2 pounds carrots, peeled and sliced (about 6 cups)
- Salt
- 6 cups chicken broth

Directions

In a heavy-bottomed pot, melt the butter. When it starts to foam, add the onions and thyme and cook over medium-low heat until tender, about 10 minutes. Add the carrots, season with salt and cook for 5 minutes. Pour in the broth, bring to a boil and then simmer until the carrots are tender, about 30 minutes. Season to taste with salt. For a smooth soup, use a blender and purée until smooth. Serves 6 to 8.

Variations

1. Garnish with crème fraîche seasoned with salt, pepper and chopped herbs.
2. Add 1/4 cup basmati rice with the carrots, use water instead of broth, add 1 cup plain yogurt just before puréeing and garnish with mint.
3. Cook a jalapeño pepper with the onions, add some cilantro before puréeing and garnish with chopped cilantro.

37824266R00041

Made in the USA
Columbia, SC
01 December 2018